A Paradox of the Life and Legacy of Coco Chanel: Power, Scandal, and the Woman Who Changed Fashion Forever

How Coco Chanel built a fashion empire, redefined femininity, and survived controversy to leave behind an unparalleled legacy

C. Fontaine Marchand

Contents

Untitled   v
As time passes, fashion changes, trends rise and fall, but Chanel remains. This book explores why.   vii

Part One
The Business Genius (How Chanel Built a Global Empire)

1. From Orphan to Icon   3
2. Breaking Fashion Norms & Creating the Chanel Empire   7
3. Chanel No. 5 – The Perfume That Changed Everything   11
4. The Reinvention Game – Chanel's Second Act at 70   16
5. Chanel After Coco – The Business That Outlived Her   20

Part Two
The Feminist Trailblazer (How She Redefined Femininity)

6. Liberating Women Through Fashion   27
7. A Woman in a Man's World   32
8. Feminist or Opportunist?   37

Part Three
The Scandal & Controversy (The Secrets of Chanel's Darkest Years)

9. Chanel & the Nazis – The Occupation Years   45
10. The Lovers, The Betrayals, and the Secret Deals   50
11. Myth vs. Reality – The Stories Chanel Told About Herself   55

Part Four
The Enduring Legacy (Why Chanel Still Matters Today)

12. The Chanel Effect – A Brand Beyond Fashion   63
13. The Chanel Manifesto: Coco Chanel's Most Iconic Quotes   68

CHANEL

*A name that signifies elegance, innovation, and controversy—**Coco Chanel** was more than a fashion designer. She was a **visionary entrepreneur**, a woman who redefined femininity, and a business strategist who built an empire in a world dominated by men*

As time passes, fashion changes, trends rise and fall, but Chanel remains. This book explores why.

Coco Chanel is a name that conjures images of timeless elegance—**the little black dress, the quilted handbag, Chanel No. 5, pearls layered with effortless sophistication.** Her influence on fashion is undisputed, but the woman behind the legend remains an enigma.

More than a designer, **Chanel was a visionary, an entrepreneur, and a force of nature.** She reshaped the way women dressed, introducing comfort, simplicity, and freedom at a time when fashion was dominated by excess and restriction. She pioneered branding before it was a concept, turning her name into a symbol of power, independence, and luxury.

But **Chanel was not without controversy.** Her life was filled with contradictions—**a self-made woman who relied on powerful men, an icon of liberation who was selective in whom she empowered, a survivor who made choices that continue to raise ethical questions.**

This book does not seek to glorify nor condemn Chanel. Instead, it aims to **tell her story in its entirety—beyond the carefully constructed myths, beyond the marketing, beyond the black-and-white narratives.**

✅ **How did she build an empire in a male-dominated world?**
✅ **How did she shape modern femininity, yet reject the label of feminism?**
✅ **How did she navigate scandal, war, and business rivalries to ensure that her name endured?**

Chanel's life was neither a fairy tale nor a tragedy. Instead, it was **a testament to reinvention, ambition, and the power of self-mythology.** She understood, better than anyone, that history remembers those who shape their own story—and she crafted hers with precision, leaving behind an empire that remains unmatched.

As time passes, fashion changes, trends rise and fall, but Chanel remains. This book explores why.

Part One
The Business Genius
(How Chanel Built a Global Empire)

From Orphan to Icon

Coco Chanel was not born into luxury. She was not raised with silk sheets, Parisian salons, or an inheritance to fund her ambitions. Instead, she began her life in a place far from the glamour she would later define—an orphanage run by nuns, where strict discipline and austerity shaped her earliest memories. These early hardships were not just obstacles to overcome; they became the foundation of her future empire.

A Childhood in Black and White

Born **Gabrielle Bonheur Chanel** on **August 19, 1883**, in **Saumur, France**, she was the second daughter of Eugénie Jeanne Devolle, a laundrywoman, and Albert Chanel, a street vendor who sold work clothes and undergarments. The Chanel family lived in poverty, constantly moving as Albert traveled from town to town in search of work. Life was unstable, and Gabrielle's childhood was marked by neglect.

Her mother's **death from tuberculosis in 1895** left the 12-year-old Gabrielle and her siblings without a caretaker. Albert Chanel, unable—or unwilling—to care for his children, sent his sons to work as farm laborers and placed Gabrielle and her sisters in **the orphanage at the Abbey of Aubazine**, a convent-run institution in central France.

At Aubazine, Gabrielle was introduced to **a world of structure, silence, and modesty.** The nuns provided shelter and education, but the environment was stark. It was here that she learned **needlework, embroidery, and sewing**—skills that would later become her gateway into fashion. The convent's strict dress code of **black and white habits**, its minimalist aesthetic, and the symmetrical architecture of the Abbey would later influence Chanel's signature **monochrome designs, clean lines, and understated luxury.**

More importantly, the orphanage taught Chanel something that would define her life: **the need for self-reliance.** She realized early that the only way to escape her fate was through reinvention.

Life After the Convent: The Making of 'Coco'

At **18, Chanel left Aubazine** and moved to **Moulins**, where she found work as a **seamstress** at Maison Grampayre, a small tailor shop. Here, she repaired and altered garments for military officers, gaining first-hand knowledge of fabric, structure, and tailoring.

But sewing alone would not elevate her to the world she aspired to join. Chanel wanted more—she wanted a life beyond the working-class limitations she was born into. **She turned to performance.**

At night, she worked at a **cabaret café, La Rotonde**, where she sang for small crowds of soldiers and wealthy patrons. Her signature song, **"Qui qu'a vu Coco?"**, a lighthearted tune about a girl searching for her lost dog, earned her the nickname *Coco*. Some claim she chose the name herself, wanting to distance herself from Gabrielle, while others suggest it was given to her by the soldiers who frequented the café.

But Coco Chanel was not destined to be a famous singer. She lacked the voice to make it on the grand stage. **What she did have, however, was an ability to charm, adapt, and captivate the right audience.**

The Turning Point: Étienne Balsan and the Entrance into High Society

It was during this time that Chanel met **Étienne Balsan**, a wealthy French ex-cavalry officer and heir to a textile fortune. Balsan was known for his lavish lifestyle, breeding racehorses and entertaining aristocrats at his estate near Compiègne. Chanel became his **mistress**, and in doing so, she gained access to a world of wealth, leisure, and connections that had been previously unimaginable to her.

At Balsan's château, **Royallieu**, Chanel observed the elite up close—their extravagance, their fashion, their mannerisms. Unlike the constrained women of working-class France, these women indulged in **silks, feathers, corsets, and jewels**. But Chanel wasn't content to simply be a spectator.

During her time at Royallieu, she began **experimenting with hats**, designing simple, elegant alternatives to the elaborate, oversized headpieces of the era. With Balsan's financial backing, she started making hats for his high-society friends. The women admired her understated, modern aesthetic—a stark contrast to the heavy, extravagant fashion of the time.

But Balsan was not Chanel's final stepping stone. Enter **Arthur "Boy" Capel.**

Arthur "Boy" Capel: The Man Who Funded Chanel's First Business

In **1909, Chanel met Arthur "Boy" Capel**, an English businessman and polo player who would become her great love and, more importantly, her first true business partner. Unlike Balsan, Capel saw Chanel not just as a mistress but as a woman with potential. **He financed her first independent venture—a hat boutique in Paris.**

With Capel's support, Chanel moved into a small apartment in Paris and set up **her first shop at 21 Rue Cambon**. She was no longer just a mistress in a man's world—she was a woman **building something of her own.**

The boutique quickly gained attention, attracting **Parisian socialites and actresses** who were drawn to Chanel's chic, minimalist hats. Her designs were unlike anything else at the time—unembellished, free of feathers, and **focused on simplicity and wearability.** This was Chanel's first rebellion against the excess of Belle Époque fashion.

But Chanel was **not content with hats alone**. She **observed the way women dressed and saw an opportunity.** Women were **restricted by corsets, layers of fabric, and ornate detailing.** Chanel wanted to free them.

The Power of Self-Mythology

By this time, Coco Chanel had fully embraced her **new identity**. Gabrielle, the orphan girl from Saumur, had vanished. In her place was *Coco*, the stylish, self-made woman who had seemingly appeared out of nowhere.

But Chanel was already rewriting her past. Throughout her life, she would claim she had never been an orphan, that her father had sent her to **live with wealthy relatives**, or that she had worked as a **governess, not a cabaret singer**. These fabrications were not just vanity—they were part of her **brand-building strategy**. Chanel understood that in order to command respect in high society, she needed a backstory that suited the image she was creating.

What mattered was not the truth, but the **illusion**.

The Rise of a Fashion Empire

Chanel's ability to **self-invent, adapt, and seize opportunity** set her apart. She was no longer an observer—she was becoming a force of her own. With **financial backing from Capel**, a rapidly growing reputation, and an innate understanding of what women wanted to wear, she was about to take the next step in her career.

She had conquered millinery. Now, she was ready to **reinvent fashion itself**.

Breaking Fashion Norms & Creating the Chanel Empire

Ambition—she was a businesswoman with a vision. Her journey from **orphan to courtesan to hat-maker** had led her to the cusp of something far greater: **revolutionizing women's fashion**.

At a time when **Parisian fashion was dominated by excess—corsets, voluminous skirts, and elaborate embellishments—**Chanel introduced a radical alternative: comfort, simplicity, and elegance. She wasn't just selling clothing; she was offering freedom. And women were ready for it.

The First Boutique: From Hats to a Fashion Revolution

With financial backing from **Arthur "Boy" Capel**, Chanel opened **her first boutique in 1910 at 21 Rue Cambon, Paris.** But there was a catch: she was only **legally allowed to sell hats** at first, since the city's strict trade laws required separate licensing for dressmaking.

The boutique, *Chanel Modes*, quickly became **a favorite among actresses and high-society women**, including **Gabrielle Dorziat** and **Émilienne d'Alençon**—both major trendsetters of the time. These women didn't just wear Chanel's hats; they **promoted them in theater productions and newspapers**, giving her exposure that money couldn't buy.

Her designs were revolutionary: gone were the heavy, feather-laden, overly adorned hats of the Belle Époque era. Instead, Chanel created **sleek, lightweight hats that exuded understated elegance**. The fashion world was beginning to take notice, but Chanel had far bigger ambitions than millinery.

By **1913**, she opened her **second boutique in Deauville, a wealthy resort town on the Normandy coast.** This was a calculated move. Deauville was a **playground for the rich**, and Chanel understood that her success depended not just on creating beautiful clothes, but on positioning them in the **right place, among the right people**.

The Birth of Casual Luxury: A New Way of Dressing

At Deauville, Chanel introduced **her first line of clothing**, marking the **official start of her career as a fashion designer**. But rather than following trends, she did something unheard of:

She used jersey fabric—previously reserved for men's underwear—to create women's dresses and sportswear.

She abandoned corsets, replacing them with loose, unstructured garments that allowed women to move freely.

She borrowed from menswear, incorporating sailor-inspired stripes, functional pockets, and relaxed silhouettes.

Jersey was **cheap and practical**, a far cry from the luxurious silks and brocades favored by high fashion at the time. But Chanel saw its potential. The fabric was **soft, flexible, and easy to wear—perfect for the modern woman.**

At first, the fashion establishment mocked her designs. They were too simple, too casual, too different. But **wealthy women loved them.**

Actresses, aristocrats, and fashionable Parisians flocked to her store, eager to embrace this **new definition of elegance—one that prioritized ease over extravagance**. Chanel wasn't just changing fashion; she was **reshaping femininity itself.**

Chanel and the War: A Business Opportunity in Crisis

In **1914, World War I broke out,** sending Europe into turmoil. Many designers, including **Paul Poiret**, who had dominated Parisian fashion before the war, struggled as their wealthy clientele disappeared. **But Chanel adapted.**

With wartime fabric shortages and rationing in place, Chanel's simple, minimalist aesthetic suddenly became **a necessity rather than just a style choice. Women were working in factories, serving as nurses, and taking on active roles outside the home. They needed practical clothing.**

Chanel's designs—**uncomplicated, comfortable, and free of unnecessary decoration—fit the moment perfectly.** While other fashion houses suffered, **Chanel's business expanded.**

By **1915,** she opened her **third boutique in Biarritz,** a coastal town known for its wealthy Spanish and British visitors. Unlike her Paris and Deauville stores, **this boutique offered haute couture—made-to-measure garments.**

Biarritz proved to be Chanel's **most profitable location yet,** and by **1916, she was running a thriving fashion house with over 300 employees.** The war had inadvertently **propelled her to the top of the industry.**

The Little Black Dress: A Symbol of Power and Rebellion

By the end of the war, Chanel had already **cemented her place in fashion,** but she was about to create her most famous design yet:

The Little Black Dress.

In 1926, *Vogue* declared **Chanel's black crepe dress with long sleeves and a simple, straight silhouette** to be "the Ford of fashion" —a reference to Henry Ford's Model T, a product known for its mass appeal and timelessness.

At the time, black was **associated with mourning,** not evening wear. But Chanel **reinvented it as a color of sophistication, mystery, and modernity.** Her philosophy?

"A woman should be two things: classy and fabulous."

Women from all social classes embraced the **LBD.** It was **affordable, elegant, and versatile**—a rare combination in high fashion.

It wasn't just a dress; it was **a statement.** It **symbolized the modern, independent woman,** unburdened by excess and convention. Decades later, Audrey Hepburn would immortalize it in *Breakfast at Tiffany's,* but it was Chanel who first made it a fashion staple.

The Rise of the Chanel Empire

By the late 1920s, Chanel was **one of the most powerful women in fashion.** Her business empire included:

A **couture house on Rue Cambon**, employing over 2,000 workers.

A **luxury perfume line**, featuring **Chanel No. 5 (introduced in 1921)**.

A line of handbags, including the famous quilted Chanel bag.

A growing list of celebrity and royal clientele, from Hollywood actresses to European aristocrats.

But **Chanel's success was not just about her designs**—it was about her ability to market them.

She instinctively understood **branding before branding even existed.** She carefully **controlled her image**, curated an air of **exclusivity**, and made sure that **wearing Chanel signified status**.

Breaking the Rules, Defining the Future

Coco Chanel didn't just **create clothes**—she **redefined fashion as a form of empowerment**. At a time when **women were expected to be decorative**, she gave them something radical:

Clothes designed for movement, not restriction.

Luxury that felt effortless, not ostentatious.

A vision of femininity that was bold, modern, and independent.

But Chanel's story was far from over. She had built a **fashion empire**, but soon she would **expand her influence even further—with the launch of a fragrance that would become the most famous perfume in history.**

Chanel No. 5 – The Perfume That Changed Everything

By the early 1920s, **Coco Chanel had already transformed women's fashion.** She had liberated women from corsets, pioneered the **little black dress**, and built a **thriving couture empire** on **Rue Cambon**. But Chanel wasn't just a designer—she was a **businesswoman with an instinct for power.**

Her next move would be **her most ambitious yet: perfume.**

Perfume, she realized, was **a unique kind of luxury**—something women could wear regardless of wealth or status. Unlike a custom-made Chanel dress, which only the elite could afford, **a bottle of perfume was an attainable indulgence.**

What she **didn't know yet** was that **Chanel No. 5** would not only become **the most famous perfume in history**, but it would also entangle her in **a decades-long business war, allegations of wartime collaboration, and a bitter fight to regain control of her empire.**

The Birth of Chanel No. 5: A Perfume Ahead of Its Time

Before Chanel, perfume was **either too delicate or too overpowering.** The most prestigious perfumes were floral-heavy and often meant for **a single social occasion—worn once and forgotten.**

But Chanel had **a different vision.**

She wanted a scent that lasted—something that lingered on a woman's skin like a second identity.

She wanted it to be complex and multi-layered, not just a single-note fragrance like rose or lavender.

She wanted it to be modern—free from the excessive sweetness and artificiality of typical perfumes.

The Role of Ernest Beaux: A Revolutionary Perfumer

To bring her vision to life, Chanel collaborated with **Ernest Beaux**, a Russian-born perfumer who had worked for the **House of Rallet**, a fragrance company that had once catered to the Russian royal family.

Beaux had been experimenting with **a groundbreaking innovation: aldehydes.**

Aldehydes were **a synthetic compound** that gave perfume **a sparkling, airy quality,** making it **crisper and longer-lasting.** Some historians believe Beaux **accidentally overdosed the aldehydes** in one of his samples, which **resulted in the distinctive, almost champagne-like freshness of Chanel No. 5.**

When Beaux presented Chanel with **a selection of samples**, she famously chose the **fifth one**—a blend of jasmine, rose, ylang-ylang, sandalwood, and a heavy dose of aldehydes.

"This is what I was waiting for," Chanel reportedly said. **"**A woman's perfume, with the scent of a woman.**"**

She named it **Chanel No. 5**, staying true to her **superstitious belief** that five was her lucky number.

The Marketing Masterstroke: How Chanel Made No. 5 a Global Sensation

Once the formula was perfected, Chanel did something **unprecedented in the perfume industry**:

She packaged it in a minimalist, rectangular glass bottle—modern, elegant, and unlike any other perfume bottle of the time.

She marketed it not as an accessory, but as **a woman's identity**—something that represented sophistication, confidence, and mystery.

She made it exclusive before making it famous—first gifting it to her wealthiest clients and Parisian elite before officially launching it.

The result? **Chanel No. 5 became a luxury icon almost instantly.**

By the **1930s**, it was being worn by Hollywood stars, European royalty, and wealthy socialites. **Marilyn Monroe's famous quote—"What do I wear to bed? Just Chanel No. 5"—**solidified its status in pop culture.

But as No. 5's success skyrocketed, so did **Chanel's conflict over its ownership.**

The Betrayal: The Wertheimer Business Deal & Chanel's Loss of Control

In **1924**, Chanel **realized she needed financial and industrial backing** to mass-produce No. 5 and expand internationally. She partnered with **Pierre and Paul Wertheimer**, Jewish businessmen who owned **Bourjois**, a leading French cosmetics and perfume company.

Under the agreement:

The Wertheimers would handle all production, marketing, and distribution.

Chanel would receive 10% of the profits.

At first, Chanel accepted the deal. But by the **1930s**, as Chanel No. 5 **became a global success, she realized she had made a mistake.**

She was **only receiving a small percentage of the millions the perfume was making**, while the Wertheimers controlled the vast majority of the profits. Furious, she tried **several times to break the contract**—but the Wertheimers, shrewd businessmen, **legally locked her out of regaining control.**

But Chanel wasn't done fighting.

World War II: Collaboration, Betrayal, and the Nazi Connection

When **Germany invaded France in 1940**, Chanel saw an **opportunity**.

During **the Nazi occupation of Paris**, Chanel used **anti-Semitic laws to try to reclaim Chanel No. 5 from the Wertheimers.** She **petitioned the Nazi government**, arguing that since the Wertheimers were Jewish, they should not be allowed to own a French business.

However, the Wertheimers had anticipated this move. **Before the war, they had legally transferred ownership of the business to a Christian business associate, Félix Amiot, ensuring that Chanel couldn't seize it.**

But Chanel's wartime activities went beyond just business. **She became romantically involved with a Nazi officer, Hans Günther von Dincklage**, a German intelligence agent. Through him, Chanel gained access to the **luxurious Ritz Hotel**, where she lived in comfort while much of Paris suffered under German rule.

After the War: Exile and a Strategic Comeback

After the war, Chanel was **arrested and questioned by French authorities for collaboration.** However, she was **never formally charged.** But the damage was done. **Chanel was seen as a collaborator, and she fled to Switzerland to avoid public backlash.** For nearly a decade, she lived in exile, with her fashion house closed and her reputation tarnished.

Winning the War for Chanel No. 5

By the early 1950s, Chanel wanted back in. At age **70**, she returned to Paris to relaunch her fashion house and **renegotiate her deal with the Wertheimers.**

In **1954**, Pierre Wertheimer **agreed to buy out all of Chanel's remaining shares**, making her **one of the richest women in France.** In exchange, **he would continue to control Chanel No. 5**—a deal that remains in place to this day.

The Wertheimer family still owns Chanel, and No. 5 continues to be one of the world's most famous perfumes.

. . .

Chanel No. 5: More Than a Perfume, A Legacy

With No. 5, Coco Chanel **didn't just create a fragrance—she created an empire.**

She redefined luxury marketing.

She turned perfume into an extension of identity.

She built a brand that, even in scandal, could not be erased.

But Chanel's fight for power was far from over. Next, she would embark on **one of the greatest comebacks in fashion history.**

The Reinvention Game – Chanel's Second Act at 70

By the early 1950s, Coco Chanel was no longer the undisputed queen of fashion.

After fifteen years in exile, her once-revolutionary aesthetic had been overshadowed by the rise of Christian Dior's "New Look," a style that reintroduced tight waists, corsets, and voluminous skirts. The look was everything Chanel had fought against—an ornate, feminine ideal that she believed was restrictive and impractical.

Dior's designs, introduced in 1947, were embraced by the fashion world, signaling a departure from the simplicity that had once defined Chanel's style. She detested the movement, famously saying, **"Dior doesn't dress women, he upholsters them."**

But fashion had moved on without her. Since Chanel had closed her couture house in 1939 at the outbreak of World War II, she had become irrelevant in the world she once ruled. The French press and elite viewed her as a traitor for her wartime associations with the Nazis, and new, younger designers were taking over the industry.

At 70 years old, many believed Chanel's career was over.

But instead of fading into obscurity, she orchestrated one of the greatest comebacks in fashion history, proving that style—and power—have no age limit.

Exile in Switzerland: The Aftermath of War

Following the liberation of Paris in 1944, Chanel was arrested and interrogated for her collaboration with the Nazis. However, she was released after only a few hours. Many believe that Winston Churchill personally intervened on her behalf, leveraging his connections with her former lover, the Duke of Westminster, one of Britain's wealthiest and most influential men.

While she had escaped legal consequences, her reputation was irreparably damaged. The public saw her as a Nazi sympathizer who had lived comfortably at the Ritz Hotel during the German occupation while others in France suffered. She had also attempted to use Nazi anti-Semitic laws to reclaim her perfume business from the Jewish Wertheimer family, an act that only added to the controversy surrounding her name.

Knowing that she was now a social pariah in France, Chanel fled to Switzerland, where she spent nearly a decade living between Lausanne and Montreux.

During her time in exile, she surrounded herself with aristocrats, aging celebrities, and former Nazi sympathizers. Though she no longer designed, she remained financially secure thanks to Chanel No. 5, which was still controlled by the Wertheimer family. The perfume remained successful worldwide, generating millions in revenue. Despite her personal animosity toward the Wertheimers, she continued to receive a percentage of the profits from the fragrance.

But exile was not enough to silence her ambition. She observed from a distance as Christian Dior's ultra-feminine designs dominated fashion, and she resented the fact that women were once again being confined by corsets and excessive fabric. She was watching, waiting, and preparing for her return.

The Grand Return: Chanel's Comeback at 70

In 1953, after 15 years away from the industry, Chanel made the bold decision to return to Paris and reopen her fashion house.

Many believed she was delusional. The industry had changed. Dior, Balmain, and Givenchy were leading the way, and Chanel was considered old-fashioned. The press and elite were still hostile toward her, and her initial return was met with skepticism.

She reopened her fashion house at **31 Rue Cambon**, determined to reestablish herself as a force in the industry. Her 1954 collection was her first attempt to challenge the dominance of Dior's New Look with a revival of her signature aesthetic—simpler, more comfortable clothing designed for movement and ease.

The reaction in France was brutal. Critics dismissed her designs as outdated and uninspired. The French press, still resentful of her wartime associations, refused to support her comeback. Her critics saw her as a relic of a past era trying to reclaim lost glory.

For a moment, it seemed as if Chanel had made a mistake.

But then something unexpected happened—the American market embraced her.

America Saves Chanel: The Rise of the Tweed Suit

The French may have rejected Chanel's comeback, but American buyers and fashion editors saw the value in her designs.

Unlike Dior's highly structured and restrictive dresses, Chanel's clothes were practical, elegant, and modern. Women who were entering the workforce in larger numbers needed outfits that allowed them to move freely. Chanel provided exactly that.

Her tweed suits became her defining look. Unlike the stiff tailoring of men's jackets, Chanel's jackets had no shoulder pads, allowing for a softer, more natural silhouette. She often used wool tweed, a fabric traditionally associated with menswear, to give women an air of effortless confidence. She added functional pockets, designed her skirts to be comfortable for movement, and focused on a timeless aesthetic rather than fleeting trends.

The Chanel suit quickly became a symbol of sophisticated independence. Women who wanted an alternative to Dior's glamorous but impractical dresses gravitated toward Chanel's understated luxury.

Hollywood stars and high-profile women adopted the look. Jacqueline Kennedy wore Chanel suits frequently, cementing their status as the epitome of refined elegance. On the day her husband, President John F. Kennedy, was assassinated in 1963, she was wearing a pink Chanel suit —a tragic moment that forever linked the design to history.

While the French had turned their backs on Chanel, the Americans had crowned her the queen of modern fashion once again.

Chanel vs. Yves Saint Laurent: A New Rivalry

By the 1960s, a new generation of designers had emerged, most notably Yves Saint Laurent.

Saint Laurent, who had taken over at Dior after Christian Dior's sudden death in 1957, introduced bold, androgynous designs, including pantsuits for women. While Chanel had borrowed from menswear, she still believed in maintaining a distinctly feminine silhouette. Saint Laurent's aesthetic went even further, fully embracing gender-fluid fashion.

Chanel was unimpressed and frequently mocked the younger designers who were gaining prominence. She saw their work as radical and impractical, believing that she alone understood what women truly wanted to wear.

Saint Laurent represented the next evolution of fashion, but Chanel's classic designs endured. Even as trends changed, her vision of timeless style remained relevant.

The Final Years: Chanel's Relentless Work Ethic

Even as she aged, Chanel never stopped working. She remained directly involved in every collection, personally approving designs and making last-minute changes. She refused to let anyone else take full creative control, ensuring that her vision remained intact.

On January 10, 1971, Coco Chanel passed away at the Ritz Hotel in Paris, where she had lived for decades. Her funeral was attended by aristocrats, celebrities, and the most influential figures in fashion, all dressed in Chanel's signature black suits.

She died alone, but her influence had already outlived her.

Chanel's Comeback: Why It Worked

Chanel's return to fashion was not just about reclaiming her place—it was about proving that reinvention was possible at any stage of life.

- She rejected fleeting trends, instead focusing on timeless design.
- She understood that simplicity, comfort, and elegance would always be in demand.
- She turned her own life story into a symbol of resilience and independence.

Chanel was not just a designer; she was an empire. And even in death, that empire would continue to grow.

Chanel After Coco – The Business That Outlived Her

When **Coco Chanel died on January 10, 1971**, at the age of 87, she left behind more than just a fashion house—she left behind an empire that was already on its way to becoming one of the most powerful luxury brands in history.

But at the time of her death, Chanel was still seen as a **traditional** and even **outdated** fashion house. Although her comeback in the 1950s had revitalized the brand, by the early 1970s, it was struggling to keep pace with a rapidly changing fashion industry. **Youth culture, ready-to-wear fashion, and the influence of designers like Yves Saint Laurent and Pierre Cardin were pushing couture into the background.**

The challenge was clear: If Chanel was to survive beyond its founder, it needed **reinvention**.

The **Wertheimer family**, who had controlled Chanel's business interests since the 1920s, recognized this. **Under their leadership, Chanel underwent a transformation that turned it into one of the most profitable and influential luxury brands of all time.**

Chanel in the 1970s: A Brand at a Crossroads

At the time of Chanel's death, the brand was in **a precarious position**.

- **The couture house was aging.** Chanel had refused to embrace new trends in the 1960s, and her style—while timeless—was losing relevance in the fast-changing world of fashion.
- **Perfume sales were strong, but the business lacked direction.** Chanel No. 5 remained **the brand's financial backbone**, but there was little expansion beyond it.
- **Chanel lacked the star power of emerging designers.** The 1970s were dominated by the likes of **Yves Saint Laurent, Halston, and Giorgio Armani**—all of whom were defining new standards for modern fashion.

For a time, **Chanel was at risk of becoming a legacy brand, a relic rather than a leader.**

But the Wertheimers had a vision.

The Wertheimer Takeover: Business First, Fashion Second

After Coco Chanel's death, control of the company fully rested with **Pierre Wertheimer** (who had secured ownership in 1954). However, Pierre was **already in his 80s** and soon passed the company on to his son, **Jacques Wertheimer**.

Jacques had **little personal interest in fashion** and was primarily focused on running the business from a financial perspective. He **invested heavily in Chanel's perfume and cosmetics division**, ensuring that No. 5 continued to dominate the fragrance market.

Throughout the 1970s, **Jacques Wertheimer largely neglected Chanel's couture business**, allowing it to **stagnate** while focusing on the brand's more profitable divisions.

Chanel couture struggled. By the early 1980s, Chanel's clothing line was producing collections that felt out of touch with the era's more dynamic and bold fashion trends. Sales had **declined dramatically**, and the house was **on the verge of becoming irrelevant**.

Enter Karl Lagerfeld: The Reinvention of Chanel

Recognizing the urgent need to revive the brand, the Wertheimers made **a pivotal decision** in 1983: They hired **Karl Lagerfeld** as the **new creative director of Chanel**.

At the time, Lagerfeld was a well-established designer known for his work with **Fendi and Chloé**, but taking over Chanel was **an enormous**

challenge. Many believed the brand was **too tied to Coco's legacy** to evolve successfully.

But Lagerfeld saw **Chanel's history not as a limitation, but as an opportunity.**

How Lagerfeld Transformed Chanel

Karl Lagerfeld's approach to Chanel was **radical yet strategic**. He understood that **Coco Chanel's designs were timeless, but the brand needed to feel modern to stay relevant.**

His key strategies included:

1. Modernizing the Chanel Suit

One of Lagerfeld's first major innovations was **revamping the Chanel suit**, a signature piece of the brand. He:

- **Shortened the skirts** to make them more youthful.
- **Added new fabrics, textures, and embellishments** while maintaining the signature tweed.
- **Introduced bold accessories**—large gold chains, statement buttons, and layered pearl necklaces.

This allowed Chanel to appeal to **a new generation** without losing its identity.

2. Expanding into Ready-to-Wear Fashion

Coco Chanel had **resisted mass production**, believing that fashion should remain in the realm of couture. Lagerfeld, however, recognized that **ready-to-wear fashion was the future**.

He launched **Chanel's first ready-to-wear collection**, making the brand **more accessible** while still maintaining an air of exclusivity.

This move **massively expanded Chanel's audience** beyond elite couture clients.

3. The Iconic Chanel Logo and Branding Strategy

Before Lagerfeld, Chanel had relied on **subtle branding**—the designs were recognizable, but they weren't covered in logos.

Lagerfeld changed this by:

- **Emphasizing the interlocking "CC" logo** on handbags, belts, jewelry, and clothing.
- **Turning Chanel into a status symbol**—something that wasn't just about fashion, but about power and exclusivity.

This was a **crucial turning point**. By making the logo a centerpiece of the brand, Lagerfeld ensured that **Chanel became an instantly recognizable luxury brand.**

4. The Rise of the Chanel Handbag Empire

While Coco Chanel had designed the famous **Chanel 2.55 bag** in 1955, it was Karl Lagerfeld who made **Chanel handbags a billion-dollar industry.**

In **1984**, he introduced the **Chanel Classic Flap Bag**, adding a **CC logo clasp** and leather-woven chain strap. The bag quickly became **one of the most coveted luxury items in the world.**

Chanel handbags became a **status symbol for celebrities, socialites, and businesswomen**, creating a new revenue stream that propelled the brand's success.

5. Reinvigorating Chanel No. 5

Although Chanel No. 5 had remained **financially successful**, its image had started to feel dated. Lagerfeld helped reposition the fragrance with **new marketing campaigns featuring high-profile celebrities** such as **Nicole Kidman and Catherine Deneuve**.

The Wertheimers also **expanded Chanel's fragrance and cosmetics division**, launching new perfumes like **Coco by Chanel (1984)** and **Allure (1996)**, which introduced younger audiences to the brand.

Chanel in the 21st Century: A Billion-Dollar Powerhouse

Karl Lagerfeld's **transformation of Chanel was a massive success.** By the 1990s and 2000s, Chanel had **secured its place as the ultimate luxury brand**, rivaling competitors like **Louis Vuitton, Hermès, and Gucci.**

Under the leadership of **Alain and Gérard Wertheimer**, the grandsons of Pierre Wertheimer, Chanel became **one of the highest-grossing privately owned fashion companies in the world.**

Today, Chanel:

• **Generates billions in annual revenue.**

• **Owns some of the most exclusive boutiques globally.**

• **Continues to dominate the perfume, fashion, and accessories market.**

After Karl Lagerfeld's **death in 2019**, Virginie Viard, his longtime collaborator, took over as creative director, continuing the brand's legacy.

Chanel's Legacy: More Than a Fashion House

Chanel is more than a clothing brand—it is **a cultural force** that has defined modern luxury.

- **It transformed fashion by embracing timeless simplicity over fleeting trends.**
- **It created one of the most recognizable and successful perfumes in history.**
- **It proved that a brand can evolve beyond its founder without losing its essence.**

Coco Chanel may have built the empire, but **it was the Wertheimers and Karl Lagerfeld who ensured it would last.**

Conclusion: Chanel's Lasting Impact

More than 50 years after Coco Chanel's death, her name **remains synonymous with elegance, power, and timeless style.**

Her influence lives on—not just in fashion, but in the way people think about **luxury, branding, and reinvention.**

The empire she built is now bigger than she could have ever imagined.

Part Two
The Feminist Trailblazer (How She Redefined Femininity)

Liberating Women Through Fashion

When **Coco Chanel** entered the fashion industry in the early 20th century, women's clothing was **dominated by rigid corsets, excessive layers, and heavy fabrics** that prioritized aesthetics over comfort. Fashion was dictated by **male designers like Paul Poiret and Charles Frederick Worth**, who largely viewed women as objects to be adorned rather than active individuals with movement, autonomy, and purpose.

Chanel changed that.

She didn't just design clothes—she **redefined what it meant to be a woman** in the modern era. Long before feminism became a mainstream movement, **her clothes embodied female liberation**. They allowed women to move, breathe, and live freely, all while maintaining elegance and sophistication.

The End of the Corset: A Revolutionary Shift in Fashion

At the turn of the 20th century, **corsets were still the norm for upper-class women.** These tight undergarments, reinforced with steel boning, cinched the waist and forced women into an **hourglass figure**, often restricting their ability to move comfortably, let alone work or participate in daily life with ease.

Early **suffragettes and progressive thinkers** had begun criticizing corsets as a **symbol of female oppression**, but mainstream fashion **was slow to adapt**.

Then came **World War I (1914–1918)**, which fundamentally changed women's roles in society. As men went off to war, **women entered the workforce in record numbers**, taking jobs in factories, offices, and hospitals. **Traditional corseted dresses were impractical for these roles**, and Chanel, recognizing this shift, stepped in with an **alternative**.

She introduced **fluid, unstructured clothing that freed the body**:
- **Soft jersey fabrics** replaced stiff, heavy materials.
- **Loose, straight silhouettes** eliminated the need for corsets.
- **Shorter hemlines** allowed for greater ease of movement.

Her designs were a **direct rejection of the restrictive fashion imposed on women for centuries**.

Chanel famously stated:

"I gave women a sense of freedom. I gave them back their bodies."

This wasn't just about style—it was a **philosophical change**.

Women could now **dress for themselves, not for the gaze of men or societal expectations**.

The Influence of Menswear: Chanel's Borrowing from Male Fashion

Chanel's second major revolution was **bringing menswear into women's fashion**.

At a time when femininity was equated with **delicate lace, bright colors, and ornate designs**, Chanel introduced **tailored blazers, striped tops, and straight-legged trousers**—garments traditionally associated with men.

Why? Because men's clothing was **practical, comfortable, and built for function**—qualities Chanel wanted to bring into women's fashion.

Her **biggest menswear-inspired innovations** included:

1. The Tweed Suit: Power Dressing Before It Existed
- Chanel's **boxy, collarless tweed jacket and matching skirt** redefined businesswear for women.

- She was inspired by **English menswear**, particularly the tweed hunting jackets worn by her lover, the Duke of Westminster.
- Unlike the corseted dresses of the past, **the suit allowed women to move freely** while still looking elegant.
- This became **the original "power suit"**, worn by professional women, aristocrats, and eventually world leaders.

2. Sailor Stripes and Nautical Fashion

- Inspired by **French sailors**, Chanel introduced the **striped Breton shirt**, originally worn by navy men.
- She made it **a symbol of casual elegance**, pairing it with **high-waisted trousers and flat shoes**—a direct challenge to the era's emphasis on delicate, impractical clothing.
- It became a wardrobe staple, later worn by **icons like Audrey Hepburn and Brigitte Bardot**.

3. The Little Black Dress: A Masculine Color Turned Feminine

- Before Chanel, **black was primarily associated with mourning and male clerical robes**.
- In 1926, she introduced **a simple, elegant black dress** in *Vogue*, describing it as **"the Ford of fashion"**—just as practical and essential as Henry Ford's automobile.
- This was a radical shift: **black was no longer just for widows—it became a statement of chic modernity.**

By incorporating elements of **masculine fashion**, Chanel subtly challenged **gender norms**, encouraging women to **dress for function rather than decoration**.

Chanel's War on Excess: Rejecting Luxury for the Sake of Luxury

At a time when **wealthy women showcased their status through elaborate gowns and heavy jewelry**, Chanel **rejected excess**.

She **eliminated the need for tight bodices, excessive beading, and heavy embroidery**, opting for a **minimalist, effortless style**.

Her fashion **wasn't about wealth—it was about attitude.**

- **Comfort was power.** A woman could now wear a suit and feel just as strong as a man.

- **Simplicity was elegance.** She believed that women didn't need over-the-top embellishments to be sophisticated.
- **Practicality was liberation.** Clothing should allow women to be active participants in life, not just decorative figures.

Her style **aligned with the growing independence of women in the 20th century**—a movement that would later be fully realized in second-wave feminism.

Was Chanel a Feminist Before Feminism?

It would be inaccurate to call Chanel **a feminist in the political sense**. She never publicly aligned herself with the **women's rights movement** and, in fact, **often distanced herself from feminist ideology.**

However, through her designs, she **embodied many of the principles of early feminism**:

✓ **She gave women freedom over their own bodies** through comfortable clothing.

✓ **She created fashion that allowed women to participate in professional life.**

✓ **She blurred the lines between "masculine" and "feminine" dress codes.**

Her work was a **precursor to the feminist fashion revolutions of the 1960s and beyond**—paving the way for designers like **Yves Saint Laurent, who introduced the first women's tuxedo, and Diane von Fürstenberg, who created the wrap dress for working women.**

Chanel didn't fight for women's rights **in speeches or protests**—she fought through **fabric, cuts, and silhouettes.**

The Critics: Did Chanel Truly Empower Women?

Despite her groundbreaking impact, **some argue that Chanel's feminism was selective**.

- **She designed for wealthy, upper-class women**, and her fashion was largely inaccessible to working-class women.
- **She was known to hold elitist and classist views**, often looking down on those who didn't fit her vision of sophistication.
- **She capitalized on women's liberation for profit** rather than actively advocating for their rights.

While she may not have been a feminist in ideology, **her legacy remains undeniable**—she changed the way women dressed, and in doing so, **changed the way they moved through the world.**

Conclusion: Fashion as Female Empowerment

Coco Chanel's designs weren't just about looking good—they were about **giving women agency, autonomy, and confidence.**

Long before the term "power dressing" existed, **Chanel had already created it.**

She **didn't just liberate women from corsets—she liberated them from societal expectations.**

A Woman in a Man's World

Coco Chanel built a **global fashion empire** at a time when the business world was almost entirely **controlled by men**. Women in the early 20th century were expected to be **wives, mothers, or socialites**—not entrepreneurs. Yet, **Chanel defied expectations**, carving out a position of power in the male-dominated worlds of fashion, business, and high society.

Her story is often told as one of pure **independence and self-made success**, but the reality is more complex. **She was both an ambitious businesswoman and a strategic networker, leveraging powerful men to advance her career.**

In this chapter, we explore:

✔ How she built a **business empire** as a self-made woman.

✔ The **role of powerful men** in her life—how they helped and how she used them.

✔ The **cost of her independence**—the compromises she made and the criticisms she faced.

Chanel's Early Career: Survival in a Male-Dominated Industry

When Chanel first entered the world of fashion, **women did not run businesses**.

• **The Parisian fashion scene was controlled by male designers** like Paul Poiret and Charles Frederick Worth.

• **Investors, bankers, and business executives were almost exclusively men.**

• **Women had little financial autonomy**—even wealthy women often depended on their fathers or husbands to handle their money.

Yet Chanel was determined to succeed on her own terms. **She didn't just want to design clothes—she wanted full control of her brand.**

But to achieve this, she **had to play by the rules of a man's world.**

Strategic Relationships: The Men Who Funded Chanel

Chanel had **several high-profile romantic relationships with powerful men**, and these connections **played a crucial role in her rise.**

Étienne Balsan: The First Step into High Society

Chanel's first serious relationship was with **Étienne Balsan**, a wealthy French textile heir and former cavalry officer.

• He introduced her to **Parisian aristocrats and wealthy women** who became her first clients.

• He provided her with **financial support** when she was starting out.

• She lived at his **estate, Royallieu**, where she began designing hats for his high-society friends.

However, Chanel **quickly outgrew her role as a kept woman** and wanted **more than financial dependence.**

Arthur "Boy" Capel: The Business Partner and True Love

Chanel's most important relationship was with **Arthur "Boy" Capel**, a wealthy English businessman and polo player.

Unlike Balsan, Capel **took Chanel seriously as an entrepreneur.**

• He **financed her first boutique in Paris** in 1910, allowing her to start her business.

- He **helped her establish the Chanel brand**, securing suppliers and advising her on business decisions.
- He **encouraged her independence**, supporting her vision even as they maintained a romantic relationship.

Capel's **tragic death in a car accident in 1919** devastated Chanel. She later said:

"Losing Capel was the only time I truly suffered."

But by this time, she had already become a **self-sustaining businesswoman**. She **used his initial investment to build something permanent—her own financial independence.**

Chanel's Business Strategy: Outmaneuvering Men in the Fashion World

Chanel was not just a designer—**she was a business strategist.**

At a time when female entrepreneurs were rare, she mastered the **art of control and branding**, ensuring that her name remained **synonymous with luxury and exclusivity.**

1. She Created a Personal Brand Before It Was Common

- Chanel understood that **a brand was more than just a product—it was a lifestyle.**
- She **became the face of her brand**, carefully cultivating an image of sophistication and independence.
- She controlled how she was **perceived in the media**, rarely allowing outsiders to dictate her narrative.

2. She Made Smart Business Deals—But Not Always in Her Favor

One of her **biggest mistakes** was **her deal with the Wertheimer family in 1924.**

- To mass-produce and distribute **Chanel No. 5**, she partnered with **Pierre Wertheimer**, giving him **70% ownership of her perfume business** in exchange for global expansion.
- At first, Chanel accepted the deal, but as No. 5 became a massive success, she realized **she had given up too much control.**
- She spent **decades trying to regain full ownership**, but the Wertheimers outmaneuvered her legally.

This was a rare instance where **Chanel underestimated the power of male businessmen**—but even in failure, she adapted, using her **royalties from No. 5 to maintain her wealth.**

The Cost of Her Independence: Power, Sacrifice, and Scandal

Chanel achieved what few women of her era did—she became **one of the richest, most influential figures in fashion**without ever marrying or relying on a man permanently.

But independence came at a price.

1. She Never Married—Was This a Choice or a Consequence?

- Chanel had **many lovers**, but she never married, claiming that she **refused to be controlled by a man**.
- However, marriage in her time **often provided women with social and financial security.**
- Some historians speculate that Chanel's **fierce independence made it difficult for her to maintain long-term relationships.**

2. She Alienated Herself From Other Women

- While Chanel designed for women, she was **not always supportive of female empowerment outside of fashion**.
- She **rarely formed close friendships with women** in business, preferring the company of male aristocrats and politicians.
- She was **known to be highly critical of other female designers**, including Elsa Schiaparelli.

3. Her WWII Controversy: A Calculated Move or a Desperate Act?

- During **World War II**, Chanel **collaborated with the Nazis**, living at the Ritz Hotel in occupied Paris.
- She attempted to **use Nazi anti-Semitic laws to take back full control of Chanel No. 5** from the Wertheimers.
- She also **became romantically involved with a Nazi intelligence officer, Hans Günther von Dincklage**, raising serious questions about her wartime loyalties.

While some argue that she **was simply trying to survive**, others see her actions as **morally indefensible.**

Her **wartime behavior permanently damaged her reputation**, and she was forced into exile in Switzerland after the war.

Chanel's Legacy: A Feminist Icon or a Self-Serving Opportunist?

Chanel's story is not a simple one.

- **She was a trailblazer**, proving that a woman could succeed in a world dominated by men.
- **She redefined power dressing**, giving women confidence through clothing.
- **She refused to be financially dependent**, building one of the most profitable fashion brands in history.

But:

- **She relied on wealthy men to launch her career** and maintain her connections.
- **She did not advocate for women's rights** outside of fashion.
- **Her wartime choices remain a point of deep controversy.**

Chanel was not a feminist **in ideology**—she never marched for women's rights or spoke about gender equality.

But in **practice**, she **lived a life of radical female independence.**

Her legacy is complex, but one truth remains:

She played the game of power better than most men of her time—and won.

Feminist or Opportunist?

Coco Chanel is often celebrated as a **feminist icon**—a woman who **redefined femininity, built a business empire, and proved that women could succeed in a male-dominated world**. Her legacy is often framed as one of **empowerment and independence**, a testament to her refusal to conform to the traditional roles of wife and mother.

But the reality is more complicated.

- Chanel never openly identified with the **women's rights movement**.
- She was known to be **elitist and dismissive of working-class women**.
- She **profited from women's liberation** but rarely **advocated for their rights outside of fashion**.
- Her **close ties with powerful men**—including Nazis during World War II—raised ethical questions about her priorities.

So, was Chanel a **pioneer for women's liberation**, or was she simply an **opportunist who used feminism when it suited her**?

In this chapter, we examine **the contradictions in her legacy**, exploring whether **her influence on women's fashion makes her a feminist figure, despite her personal beliefs and actions.**

. . .

Chanel and Feminism: A Complicated Relationship

Chanel's impact on **women's clothing and social mobility** was undeniable.

• She **freed women from restrictive corsets**, creating **practical, comfortable fashion that allowed for movement and independence**.

• She introduced **menswear-inspired designs**, redefining **how women dressed for work and daily life**.

• She proved that a **woman could build and control a global brand** without being financially dependent on a husband.

These achievements align with many **feminist principles**, but Chanel **never openly supported the feminist movement**.

Throughout her life, she was **indifferent, if not dismissive, of political activism**.

In contrast to **designers like Elsa Schiaparelli**, who embraced progressive ideas and worked closely with avant-garde feminist circles, **Chanel avoided aligning herself with any ideological movement.**

Her philosophy was **not about equality**—it was about **power**. She once said:

"I don't care what you think of me. I don't think about you at all."

This quote, while reflective of her fierce independence, also underscores her **lack of interest in collective struggles for women's rights.**

Chanel may have **empowered women through fashion**, but she was **not a feminist in the political sense**.

Chanel's Elitism: Did She Truly Liberate All Women?

Another contradiction in Chanel's supposed feminism was her **classism**.

While she revolutionized fashion, her designs **were not accessible to all women**.

• **Chanel's clothing was designed for the wealthy.** Her suits and dresses were worn by **aristocrats, celebrities, and high-society women**—not by the working-class women who had little access to luxury fashion.

• **She looked down on the poor.** Despite coming from an orphanage, she had **no real empathy for working-class women**, preferring the company of the aristocracy.

• **She maintained an air of exclusivity.** Even today, Chanel's designs remain a **symbol of privilege rather than accessibility.**

Unlike designers such as **Madeleine Vionnet**, who sought to create fashion that celebrated the natural female form for women of all backgrounds, Chanel's vision was **closely tied to wealth and social status.**

Her success may have **shattered gender barriers**, but **it did not dismantle class barriers.**

Her fashion may have freed women **physically**, but it was **only available to those who could afford it.**

The Men in Chanel's Life: Independence or Strategic Dependence?

Chanel's image as a **self-made woman** is somewhat misleading.

While she was undoubtedly **brilliant, talented, and fiercely independent**, she **relied on powerful men to advance her career.**

• **Étienne Balsan provided her with financial security in her early years.**

• **Arthur "Boy" Capel funded her first boutique and shaped her business strategy.**

• **The Wertheimer family controlled and financed Chanel No. 5, making her millions.**

• **The Duke of Westminster introduced her to high society, securing wealthy clients.**

Chanel **never married**, and she built her empire without a husband. But she was **not entirely self-sufficient**—she **leveraged relationships with powerful men to gain access to wealth and influence.**

While this was a **survival strategy in a male-dominated world**, it also raises questions:

- Was Chanel's **independence real**, or was it **carefully curated through male sponsorship?**
- Would she have succeeded **without these men** backing her financially and socially?

She **outmaneuvered men in business**, but she also **relied on them when necessary.**

This makes her **both a feminist figure and an opportunist**, depending on how one views her use of power.

The Nazi Collaboration: A Betrayal of Feminist Ideals?
One of the most controversial aspects of Chanel's legacy is **her actions during World War II.**

- She **lived at the Ritz Hotel in Nazi-occupied Paris** while many Parisians suffered under German rule.
- She **had a romantic relationship with Nazi intelligence officer Hans Günther von Dincklage.**
- She **attempted to use Nazi anti-Semitic laws to seize full control of Chanel No. 5 from the Jewish Wertheimer family.**
- She was **allegedly involved in Nazi intelligence operations**, acting as **Agent F-7124** under the codename "Westminster."

While some argue that **she did what she had to do to survive**, others believe her choices **went beyond self-preservation and into collaboration.**

If Chanel was truly an advocate for women, **why did she not use her influence to help those suffering under Nazi rule?**

Many **female resistance fighters risked their lives to fight against fascism**, yet Chanel **aligned herself with Nazi officers.**

This raises difficult ethical questions:
- **Did Chanel betray the very women she claimed to empower?**
- **Does her wartime behavior disqualify her from being seen as a feminist figure?**

Even after the war, Chanel **never expressed regret** for her actions. Unlike other public figures who were forced to reckon with their collaboration, she **escaped any real consequences**—likely due to her connections with Winston Churchill and the Duke of Westminster.

This part of her history remains **a stain on her legacy**, complicating any narrative of her as a feminist icon.

How Modern Feminism Views Chanel

Today, Chanel's legacy is **divisive.**

Some feminists celebrate her as **a pioneer who gave women freedom through fashion and proved that a woman could build a global empire.**

Others criticize her as **a privileged opportunist who used power for personal gain rather than for the advancement of women.**

Her influence on **women's clothing is undeniable**, but her **political and ethical choices remain troubling.**

The Case for Chanel as a Feminist Icon:

✓ She **freed women from corsets and rigid fashion expectations.**

✓ She **created fashion that allowed women to move, work, and live more freely.**

✓ She **built a powerful business in a time when women had little control over money or industry.**

The Case Against Chanel as a Feminist:

✗ She **never actively fought for women's rights outside of fashion.**

✗ She **collaborated with Nazi officers and used anti-Semitic laws for personal gain.**

✗ She **relied on relationships with wealthy men to build her empire.**

Ultimately, **Chanel's legacy exists in shades of gray.**

She was not a feminist in the way we think of the term today—but she **lived a life that embodied many feminist principles** long before they were widely accepted.

She **empowered women, but she did not fight for them.**

She **broke barriers, but she did not try to bring others with her.**

Her story is one of **contradictions—an inspiring tale of independence, power, and innovation, tainted by self-interest and moral ambiguity.

Conclusion: The Chanel Paradox
Coco Chanel was both:

✔ A visionary who changed women's lives through fashion.

✘ A self-serving opportunist who prioritized her survival over ethics.

Her legacy is complicated, but one thing is clear:

She defined modern femininity—not with words, but with fabric, style, and ambition.

Part Three
The Scandal & Controversy (The Secrets of Chanel's Darkest Years)

Chanel & the Nazis – The Occupation Years

Coco Chanel's wartime years remain **one of the most controversial chapters of her life.** Between **1940 and 1944,** she lived in **Nazi-occupied Paris**, resided at the **Ritz Hotel**, and maintained a **romantic relationship with a high-ranking Nazi officer.**

For decades, her defenders claimed she was simply **a woman caught in the wrong place at the wrong time**, a **fashion designer trying to survive the war**. But emerging historical evidence suggests her involvement may have gone beyond mere survival.

- Did Chanel actively collaborate with the Nazis?
- Did she attempt to use Nazi anti-Semitic laws to seize full control of Chanel No. 5?
- Why did she escape prosecution when many others accused of collaboration were arrested or executed?

In this chapter, we examine **the evidence, counterarguments, and lasting consequences** of her actions during World War II.

Paris Under Nazi Occupation: Life at the Ritz

In **June 1940**, the German army **invaded France**, and within weeks, **Paris fell under Nazi control**. The once-glamorous city was transformed into a **divided, fearful place**.

• The Nazi military **commandeered luxury hotels, restaurants, and stores**, turning Paris into a city of **privilege for high-ranking German officials** while the general population **suffered from food shortages, curfews, and oppression**.

• **The Ritz Hotel**, located in the heart of Place Vendôme, became the headquarters for **top Nazi officers and intelligence agents**.

Chanel, who had been **living at the Ritz before the war**, remained there **throughout the entire German occupation**.

This fact alone is **highly incriminating**—the Ritz was **not a place where ordinary Parisians could stay under Nazi rule. Only those with close ties to the Germans had access**.

During this period, **Chanel became romantically involved with Baron Hans Günther von Dincklage**, a **senior intelligence officer in the Nazi Abwehr (military intelligence)**.

Von Dincklage had previously been a **propaganda agent in the Third Reich and was known for recruiting informants in occupied France**. His relationship with Chanel gave her **protection, privilege, and security**—while many of her fellow Parisians suffered under the occupation.

Some historians argue that **Chanel's presence at the Ritz and her relationship with von Dincklage indicate more than passive survival—they suggest collaboration.**

Operation Modellhut: Chanel's Alleged Role in Nazi Intelligence

In **2011**, newly declassified documents from **French wartime intelligence services** revealed that **Coco Chanel had been registered as a Nazi intelligence agent** under the codename **"Westminster"**—a reference to her past lover, the Duke of Westminster.

The documents indicate that:

• Chanel was **Agent F-7124** in the Abwehr.

• She was **involved in a German intelligence operation known as "Modellhut" (Operation Model Hat)**.

• The goal of the operation was to **establish secret peace negotiations between the Nazis and Britain—with Chanel acting as a courier between German intelligence and her high-society British contacts.

In **1943**, Chanel **traveled to Madrid** with von Dincklage and met with a known German spy, **Walter Schellenberg**, and the British ambassador, Sir Samuel Hoare.

The mission was **a failure**—the British government refused to negotiate with Nazi Germany—but Chanel's role in it **raised serious ethical and political questions.**

- **Was she ideologically aligned with the Nazis?**
- **Or was she simply trying to position herself on the winning side of the war?**

Chanel never spoke publicly about this episode. She neither denied nor confirmed her involvement, allowing speculation and uncertainty to define her wartime legacy.

Betraying the Wertheimer Family: Chanel's Use of Anti-Semitic Laws

Perhaps the most damning evidence of **Chanel's opportunism during the war** was her **attempt to exploit Nazi anti-Semitic laws to take back control of Chanel No. 5.**

Since **1924**, Chanel No. 5 had been controlled by the **Wertheimer brothers**, Pierre and Paul, who had legally secured **70% of the business** in exchange for producing and distributing the perfume globally.

During the Nazi occupation, **France's Vichy government enacted Aryanization laws**, which stripped Jewish business owners of their rights. Chanel saw an **opportunity**.

- She **petitioned the Vichy authorities**, claiming that, as an "Aryan," she should be granted **sole ownership of Parfums Chanel**.
- She wrote a **formal letter to German administrators**, citing her previous deal with the Wertheimers as **unfair and illegal under Nazi racial laws**.

What she **didn't know** was that **the Wertheimers had already anticipated this move.**

Before fleeing France, **they transferred legal ownership of their**

business to a Christian businessman, **Félix Amiot**, ensuring that **Chanel couldn't seize their company** under Nazi rule.
- **Chanel's attempt to steal the company failed.**
- **The Wertheimers ultimately regained control of Chanel No. 5 after the war.**
- **They later settled financially with Chanel, granting her continued profits from the perfume.**

This episode is one of **the darkest stains on Chanel's legacy**—it was **not just collaboration for survival, but an active attempt to profit from Nazi policies.**

The Liberation of Paris: How Chanel Escaped Punishment

In **August 1944**, Paris was liberated from Nazi rule. French citizens who had collaborated with the Germans were **publicly humiliated, arrested, or executed.**
- Women accused of "horizontal collaboration" (romantic relationships with Nazis) were paraded through the streets with shaved heads.
- **Businesspeople who had profited from the occupation were put on trial.**
- **Some were imprisoned; others were executed for treason.**

Chanel was briefly **arrested by the French Forces of the Interior (FFI)** but was released after **just a few hours of questioning.**

Why?

Many believe **Winston Churchill intervened,** using his influence to protect her. Churchill had been **a close friend of the Duke of Westminster**, one of Chanel's most powerful former lovers. It is widely suspected that he pressured the French authorities to **drop the case against her.**

Unlike other suspected collaborators, **Chanel faced no formal charges.**

However, she knew her **position in France was no longer tenable**. She fled to **Switzerland**, where she lived in exile for nearly a decade, avoiding the public backlash that followed the war.

. . .

After the War: A Strategic Comeback

By the 1950s, Chanel saw an opportunity to **return to Paris and revive her fashion house**.

- She **rebranded herself, avoiding any public discussion of her wartime activities**.
- She cultivated **an image of resilience**, portraying herself as a **victim of war rather than a collaborator**.
- She resumed **her business partnership with the Wertheimers**, who **forgave her wartime betrayal and continued producing Chanel No. 5**.

Her comeback was met with **skepticism in France** but **enthusiasm in America**, where her past was less scrutinized.

By **the 1960s**, she had **successfully rewritten her own history**—focusing on **her contributions to fashion while burying the darker parts of her legacy**.

Conclusion: Was Chanel a Nazi Collaborator or a Survivor?

The truth is complex.

- **She lived among Nazi officials in the Ritz while the rest of France suffered.**
- **She had a Nazi lover and worked with German intelligence.**
- **She attempted to use Nazi laws for personal gain.**
- **Yet she avoided any real consequences after the war.**

Chanel was not an ideological Nazi—but **she was an opportunist** who **chose personal survival and profit over moral integrity**.

Her wartime choices remain **one of the most damning aspects of her legacy**, proving that **her ambition knew no ethical boundaries.**

The Lovers, The Betrayals, and the Secret Deals

The Lovers, The Betrayals, and the Secret Deals

Coco Chanel was **a master strategist**—not just in fashion but in life. She built her empire not only through talent and business acumen but also through **carefully cultivated relationships with powerful men** who provided her with the financial backing, social connections, and strategic advantages she needed to succeed.

Yet, just as Chanel **used others to rise**, she was also **capable of betrayal**. Few stories in fashion history are as **ruthless** as Chanel's attempt to **seize full control of Chanel No. 5 by exploiting Nazi anti-Semitic laws**. And despite this betrayal, she somehow managed to **make peace with her business partners and secure her financial future** after the war.

In this chapter, we examine:

✔ Her powerful lovers—from aristocrats to Nazi officers—and how they shaped her rise.

✔ How she leveraged relationships to gain influence and financial backing.

✔ Her controversial battle for Chanel No. 5, including her attempted betrayal of her Jewish business partners.

Love, Power, and Influence: The Men Who Shaped Chanel's Rise

Chanel never married. She was fiercely independent and **rejected the idea of being "owned" by a man**. But she also understood that **men controlled money, business, and politics**—and that relationships could provide her with opportunities that would otherwise be impossible.

Her lovers were not ordinary men. They were **aristocrats, political figures, military officers, and industrialists**—men who could introduce her to the **right circles, secure financing, and provide protection when needed**.

Étienne Balsan: Chanel's Entry into High Society

Chanel's first major romantic partner was **Étienne Balsan**, an ex-cavalry officer from a wealthy French textile family.

- He introduced Chanel to **the world of aristocratic leisure**, where she first encountered the women who would become her early clients.
- He supported her **financially**, allowing her to live in luxury at his country estate, Royallieu.
- She began designing hats for **Balsan's wealthy friends**, marking the **first step in her career.**

Yet, Chanel **grew frustrated with Balsan's lack of ambition**. She wanted more than **a life as a mistress in a man's estate**. So, she left him—for a man who **offered her something greater than comfort: investment.**

Arthur "Boy" Capel: The Business Partner and Lover Who Built Chanel

Chanel's most significant lover was **Arthur "Boy" Capel**, a wealthy English businessman and polo player.

Unlike Balsan, Capel **saw Chanel's potential and took her ambitions seriously**.

- He **funded the opening of her first boutique in 1910**, marking the real beginning of the Chanel fashion house.
- He advised her on **business strategy and branding**, helping her navigate the male-dominated world of fashion.

- He encouraged her **to expand beyond hats and create a full fashion line.**

Chanel was deeply in love with Capel, but **he never married her**—instead, he married an aristocratic Englishwoman.

In 1919, Capel **died tragically in a car accident**, leaving Chanel devastated. She later admitted:

"Losing Capel was the only time I truly suffered."

Yet, by this point, **Chanel had become self-sufficient**—thanks largely to the financial and strategic support Capel had provided.

The Duke of Westminster: A Brush with British Royalty

In the 1920s, Chanel had a long affair with **Hugh Grosvenor, the 2nd Duke of Westminster**, one of Britain's wealthiest men.

- He **lavished her with wealth and properties**, including a home in the French Riviera.
- He introduced her to **British high society**, including Winston Churchill.
- She was influenced by **British country fashion**, which later inspired her famous tweed suits.

Westminster eventually wanted to marry Chanel, but she refused. She later said:

"There have been many Duchesses of Westminster. There is only one Chanel."

Despite the relationship ending, **Chanel's ties to British aristocracy would later prove useful when she needed protection after World War II.**

Hans Günther von Dincklage: The Nazi Officer Who Ensured Chanel's Wartime Privileges

During World War II, Chanel became **romantically involved with Hans Günther von Dincklage**, a high-ranking German intelligence officer.

- He was a **Nazi spy**, working directly under German military intelligence.
- Their relationship gave **Chanel protection during the occupation**, allowing her to **live at the Ritz Hotel in Nazi-occupied Paris** while others suffered.

- He helped her **navigate Nazi bureaucracy**, particularly in her attempt to seize control of Chanel No. 5.

This relationship remains **one of the most damning aspects of Chanel's wartime history**. She later downplayed its significance, but the fact remains:
- **Von Dincklage was an active Nazi intelligence agent.**
- **Chanel benefited from their relationship while many others in France were persecuted.**

After the war, **her ties to British aristocracy likely saved her from prosecution**, as Winston Churchill is believed to have **intervened to protect her from post-war trials**.

The Betrayal of the Wertheimers: Chanel's Battle for Chanel No. 5

The 1924 Deal: The Agreement She Would Regret

In **1924**, Chanel made a business deal with **Pierre Wertheimer**, a Jewish businessman who owned **Bourjois**, a successful French cosmetics company.
- Wertheimer provided **the capital and distribution infrastructure** needed to mass-produce **Chanel No. 5**.
- In exchange, he took **70% ownership of Parfums Chanel**, leaving Chanel with only **10%**.

At the time, this seemed like a fair deal—**Chanel lacked the resources to manufacture perfume on her own**.

But as **Chanel No. 5 became the most successful fragrance in the world**, she realized that she had **given up too much control**.

By the 1930s, Chanel **despised the Wertheimers**, calling them "Jewish businessmen" who had taken advantage of her. She began **seeking ways to regain full ownership**.

The Wartime Betrayal: Using Nazi Anti-Semitic Laws

When the Nazis occupied France in **1940**, they implemented **Aryanization laws**, which stripped Jewish business owners of their assets.

Seeing an opportunity, **Chanel petitioned the Vichy government, claiming that as an Aryan, she had the right to seize full control of Parfums Chanel from the Jewish Wertheimer family.

However, what **Chanel didn't know** was that **the Wertheimers had already anticipated this move.**

Before fleeing France, they **transferred control of Parfums Chanel to Félix Amiot**, a non-Jewish businessman, ensuring that Chanel could not legally take over the company.

Her attempt to **exploit Nazi laws for financial gain failed**—but the betrayal was undeniable.

Post-War Settlement: The Wertheimers Save Chanel's Business

After the war, Chanel's **image was tarnished**, and she had **no way to regain full control of Chanel No. 5.**

Yet, in an ironic twist, **Pierre Wertheimer ended up saving her career.**

• In **1954**, Chanel and Wertheimer negotiated a new deal:

  ◦ She **would continue receiving royalties from Chanel No. 5**.

  ◦ Wertheimer **would finance the reopening of her fashion house**, allowing her to stage her **1954 comeback.**

Despite her wartime betrayal, Wertheimer recognized that **Chanel's brand still had value**. Instead of punishing her, he ensured that **she remained financially comfortable for the rest of her life.**

Conclusion: A Woman Who Played the Game Ruthlessly

Coco Chanel's life was filled with **strategic alliances, betrayals, and power plays**.

• **She used men to build her empire—but never let them own her.**

• **She attempted to betray her Jewish business partners, yet ultimately relied on them to restore her career.**

• **She survived scandals that would have destroyed others—because she knew how to make herself indispensable.**

Her legacy is one of **brilliance and cold calculation**, proving that Chanel was not just a designer—**she was a survivor.**

Myth vs. Reality – The Stories Chanel Told About Herself

Coco Chanel was not just a designer—she was a storyteller, a woman who understood the power of image and reinvention. She built more than a fashion empire; she crafted a **personal myth** that blurred the lines between truth and fiction.

Many great historical figures have carefully shaped their own legacies, but Chanel was particularly masterful at it. Through interviews, selective memories, and omissions, she ensured that the world saw **only what she wanted it to see**.

Some of these fabrications were meant to **strengthen her personal legend**, while others were designed to **protect her from scrutiny**—especially when it came to **her wartime activities**.

In this chapter, we separate **fact from fiction**, uncovering:

✔ How she reshaped her childhood into a dramatic survival story.

✔ The exaggerations and omissions surrounding her rise in fashion.

✔ The contradictions in her personal and business life.

✔ The truths she carefully concealed about World War II.

. . .

Chanel's Childhood: A Story She Rewrote
The Myth: The Abandoned Orphan Who Rose from Nothing

Chanel often **presented herself as an orphan**, abandoned by her father after the death of her mother. She claimed to have **grown up in extreme poverty**, struggling through a difficult childhood without support.

She used this narrative to reinforce her **self-made success**, presenting herself as a woman who had to fight for everything she achieved.

In later years, she also suggested that her **years in the convent orphanage instilled in her a sense of discipline and simplicity**, which would later influence her **minimalist design philosophy**.

The Reality: A More Complicated Family History

While Chanel's childhood was undeniably difficult, it was not as **dramatic as she later claimed**.

- Chanel's mother, **Jeanne Devolle**, died of tuberculosis when Chanel was **12 years old**.
- Her father, **Albert Chanel**, did not completely abandon her. Instead, **he left her and her sisters in the care of a Catholic orphanage at the Abbey of Aubazine** while he worked to support himself.
- While life at the orphanage was strict, Chanel **received an education** there—learning **sewing, embroidery, and discipline**, skills that would later serve her well.

So why did she **alter the details**?

The story of **a poor orphan girl rising from nothing** was far more powerful than the reality of a **child from modest means who still had some family connections and opportunities**.

By removing the nuances of her past, Chanel made her **success appear even more extraordinary**.

Her Rise in Fashion: Was She Truly Self-Made?
The Myth: A Woman Who Built Her Empire Alone

Chanel always insisted that she **achieved success entirely on her**

own, through sheer determination and talent. She often downplayed or ignored **the role of others—especially men—in shaping her career.**

The Reality: A Combination of Talent, Strategy, and Support

Chanel's ability to **design and innovate** was **undeniable**, but she also **benefited greatly from key relationships**.

- **Étienne Balsan**, her first serious partner, introduced her to **high society** and provided **financial support** in her early years.
- **Arthur "Boy" Capel** not only financed **her first boutique in 1910**, but also **helped her establish the business principles** that would guide her company.
- **Pierre Wertheimer**, despite their later disputes, was instrumental in **turning Chanel No. 5 into a global success**.

Why did Chanel **minimize these contributions**?

- She preferred to **emphasize her independence**, a quality that became **central to her brand identity**.
- Admitting that men played a role in her rise might have **weakened the image of the strong, self-sufficient woman she projected**.

The reality is that **Chanel was both independent and strategic—**she knew how to align herself with the right people, but she also had the **vision and ambition to make the most of those opportunities**.

Chanel and World War II: The Silence That Followed

The Myth: An Innocent Bystander in a Dangerous Time

After World War II, Chanel **avoided discussing her activities during the war**. She insisted that she had been **apolitical**, uninterested in collaborating with any regime.

She suggested that she had merely been a **fashion designer trying to survive**, like many others in occupied Paris.

For years, this version of events was accepted—partly because **Chanel was never formally charged with collaboration** and partly because **she controlled her own narrative** in the media.

The Reality: A More Complex and Controversial Story

The **release of declassified French intelligence documents in 2011** confirmed that **Chanel had direct ties to German intelligence**.

- She was **registered as an agent of the Nazi military intelligence unit, the Abwehr**, under the codename **"Westminster"**.
- She had **a close relationship with Nazi intelligence officer Hans Günther von Dincklage**, who provided her with **privileges at the Ritz Hotel during the occupation.**
- She participated in **Operation Modellhut**, a failed Nazi intelligence mission aimed at negotiating peace with Britain.

Most controversially, Chanel **attempted to use Nazi anti-Semitic laws to take full control of Chanel No. 5** from the Jewish Wertheimer family. However, **her plan failed** because the Wertheimers had **preemptively transferred ownership of the company to a Christian business associate, Félix Amiot** before fleeing France.

Why Did She Escape Consequences?

Unlike other high-profile collaborators who were arrested, publicly humiliated, or even executed, **Chanel faced no formal punishment**.

Possible reasons include:

- **Her powerful British connections**, particularly **Winston Churchill**, who may have intervened on her behalf.
- Her **long period of exile in Switzerland after the war**, which allowed time for public memory to fade.
- A **post-war focus on rebuilding France**, which led to selective prosecution of collaborators.

By the time she returned to Paris in the 1950s, Chanel had **successfully distanced herself from her wartime past** and rebranded herself as a **fashion legend, not a political figure**.

Chanel's Public Persona: The Contradictions She Created

Even in personal matters, Chanel **crafted a version of herself** that sometimes conflicted with reality.

1. Her Age

- Chanel often **lied about her birth year**, making herself appear **younger than she really was**.
- She claimed to have been born in **1893**, but records confirm she was born in **1883**.

This small deception helped her **maintain the image of an ageless icon**.

2. Her Relationships

- She **romanticized her love for Boy Capel**, even though their relationship was **complicated and largely pragmatic**.
- She **never spoke publicly about her affair with von Dincklage**, despite its well-documented existence.

3. Her Attitude Toward Wealth

- Chanel often claimed to **reject wealth and excess**, yet she **lived in luxury, surrounded by riches**.
- She described herself as an **anti-materialist**, yet was **obsessed with financial control**.

Conclusion: Who Was the Real Coco Chanel?

Chanel was a woman of **contradictions**—fiercely independent, yet deeply reliant on powerful men; politically disengaged, yet connected to wartime intelligence; a champion of women's liberation in fashion, yet largely uninterested in feminism as a movement.

She **shaped her own story**, ensuring that **she would be remembered not just for what she did, but for how she wanted to be seen.**

Even today, separating **fact from fiction** in her life remains challenging.

What is undeniable, however, is that **her influence on fashion and culture endures**.

She was not perfect, nor was she purely villainous. **She was, above all, a survivor and a visionary—one who understood that history is written by those who know how to tell their own story.**

Final Thoughts: The Legacy of Chanel

Was Chanel a hero? A pragmatist? A survivor? A visionary?

The answer is: **She was all of these things at once.**

Her story is one of **ambition, resilience, and reinvention**, and even as history examines her more critically, **her legacy remains as influential as ever.**

Part Four
The Enduring Legacy (Why Chanel Still Matters Today)

The Chanel Effect – A Brand Beyond Fashion

Coco Chanel has been **gone for over fifty years**, yet her influence on **fashion, branding, and culture remains unparalleled**. The world she left behind—one of mass production, rapidly shifting trends, and changing standards of beauty—should have made her legacy obsolete. Instead, **Chanel remains one of the most recognizable and profitable luxury brands in the world.**

But Chanel's **enduring relevance** goes beyond fashion.
• Her approach to branding revolutionized the luxury industry.
• Her aesthetic continues to define modern femininity.
• Her contradictions—both inspiring and controversial—spark ongoing debates about ethics, feminism, and history.

This chapter explores **how Chanel's influence still permeates fashion, culture, and business today**, while also examining the **moral complexities of idolizing a figure who was both a trailblazer and a pragmatist who made questionable choices.**

Chanel's Impact on Fashion: Simplicity as Power

Coco Chanel's **most radical idea** was that **style should be effortless**. At a time when high fashion was defined by **excess and decoration**, she introduced an aesthetic of **minimalism and practicality** that still defines modern luxury.

1. The Chanel Suit: Power Dressing for Generations

The **Chanel suit**, introduced in the 1920s and refined in the 1950s, remains **a symbol of power and sophistication**.

- **Jackie Kennedy wore it.**
- **Princess Diana wore it.**
- **Modern celebrities and businesswomen still wear it.**

Even today, designers frequently **reinterpret the Chanel suit**, proving that its influence has never faded.

2. The Little Black Dress: A Staple in Every Woman's Closet

Before Chanel, **black was for mourning**. She transformed it into **a symbol of sophistication, independence, and effortless elegance**.

- The **LBD (Little Black Dress)** is now a **must-have** in every wardrobe.
- It remains the go-to choice for **cocktail events, business meetings, and even casual occasions.**
- It embodies Chanel's philosophy: **elegance that is simple, timeless, and powerful.**

3. Chanel No. 5: The World's Most Iconic Perfume

Since its launch in **1921, Chanel No. 5** has remained one of the **best-selling and most recognizable perfumes** in history.

Why? Because Chanel understood **the power of branding and exclusivity.**

- She created the **first perfume associated with a fashion house.**
- She used **minimalist packaging and a sleek glass bottle**, making it feel modern and luxurious.
- She turned **celebrity endorsements into an art form**—Marilyn Monroe famously declared she wore only "Chanel No. 5" to bed.

Even in the **era of influencer marketing**, Chanel No. 5 **remains relevant**, proving that a carefully crafted brand can last generations.

. . .

Chanel's Impact on Modern Feminism: Style as Liberation

Chanel never **called herself a feminist**, yet her work **fundamentally changed how women dressed and moved through the world**.

- She rejected **corsets and restrictive clothing**, allowing women to move freely.
- She introduced **trousers, suits, and flat shoes**, giving women a wardrobe that matched their growing independence.
- She proved that **a woman could control her own business, brand, and finances** at a time when few did.

Chanel's Influence on Today's Feminist Fashion

Her ideas are reflected in **contemporary fashion trends**:

- **Athleisure and comfort-driven fashion** owe their existence to her philosophy that clothing should prioritize ease and function.
- **Power dressing in the workplace**—from blazers to sleek monochrome looks—follows Chanel's belief that elegance should be effortless.
- **Gender-neutral and androgynous fashion** borrows from Chanel's early incorporation of menswear into women's wardrobes.

Chanel's core message—that **women's clothing should be beautiful but never restrictive**—continues to shape modern fashion.

The Ethics of Idolizing Chanel: Should Her Scandals Matter?

While Chanel's **fashion legacy is undeniable**, her **personal history remains deeply complicated**.

The Argument for Separating Art from the Artist

Many argue that Chanel's **work should stand on its own**, separate from her personal life.

- Her designs liberated women.
- She built an empire that outlived her.
- Her contributions to branding, luxury, and fashion are still relevant.

From this perspective, **her moral failings**—including her wartime choices—should not overshadow her artistic contributions.

The Argument for Holding Chanel Accountable

However, others believe that **Chanel's past cannot be ignored**.

- Her **ties to the Nazis during World War II** raise ethical concerns about her **collaboration and self-preservation.**
- She **attempted to use anti-Semitic laws** to seize full control of Chanel No. 5.
- Her **elitist views and dismissive attitude toward feminism** contradict the progressive image often attributed to her.

Some ask: **Should we continue idolizing a figure with such a morally complex history?**

The debate reflects a broader question in modern culture: **Can we celebrate a person's achievements while acknowledging their flaws?**

Why Chanel Remains an Icon in the 21st Century

Despite these debates, **Chanel's influence remains as strong as ever.**

1. The Chanel Brand Continues to Thrive

- Under the leadership of **Karl Lagerfeld (1983–2019)**, the house of Chanel expanded into **ready-to-wear fashion, handbags, and global markets**.
- Today, under **Virginie Viard**, Chanel remains one of the most **successful luxury brands**, worth **billions of dollars**.

2. Chanel's Aesthetic Is Timeless

Fashion is cyclical, yet Chanel's core elements—**black and white, tweed, pearls, structured silhouettes**—remain **eternally stylish**.

- Unlike **trend-driven brands**, Chanel built a **signature aesthetic that never feels outdated.**
- Even as fashion shifts, **Chanel remains a benchmark for elegance and sophistication.**

3. Chanel's Message Still Resonates

At its core, Chanel's philosophy was simple:
"Fashion fades, only style remains the same."

This belief—**that confidence, individuality, and simplicity define true beauty**—continues to inspire new generations.

In a world dominated by **fast fashion and fleeting trends,**

Chanel's insistence on **quality, craftsmanship, and timeless design** has made her brand more relevant than ever.

Final Thoughts: The Chanel Paradox

Coco Chanel's life was filled with **contradictions**—she was innovative yet traditional, rebellious yet calculated, a liberator yet deeply pragmatic.

- She **reshaped fashion** but was **not a political feminist.**
- She **created a timeless brand** but **made questionable choices in her personal and business dealings.**
- She **built her own legend**, ensuring that her influence would never fade, even after her death.

Should We Still Celebrate Chanel?

That is **a question every individual must answer for themselves.**

Her legacy is neither **purely heroic nor entirely villainous**—it is complex, nuanced, and deeply human.

What cannot be denied is that **Chanel changed the way women dress, the way luxury brands operate, and the way history remembers those who shape culture.**

Even today, when we see a **black dress, a quilted handbag, or a tweed suit**, we are reminded of **Coco Chanel's lasting imprint on the world.**

The Chanel Manifesto: Coco Chanel's Most Iconic Quotes

On Fashion & Style

"Fashion fades, only style remains the same."

- Dress shabbily and they remember the dress; dress impeccably and they remember the woman."
- Simplicity is the keynote of all true elegance."
- "A girl should be two things: classy and fabulous."
- "Fashion is architecture: it is a matter of proportions."
- "Luxury must be comfortable, otherwise it is not luxury."
- "A woman can be overdressed but never over-elegant."
- "Adornment, wha

t a science! Beauty, what a weapon! Modesty, what elegance!"

On Femininity & Empowerment

- "I don't care what you think about me. I don't think about you at all."

- *You live but once; you might as well be amusing."*
- *"The most courageous act is still to think for yourself. Aloud."*
- *"A woman who doesn't wear perfume has no future."*
- *"If you're sad, add more lipstick and attack."*
- *"A woman with good shoes is never ugly."*
- *"I don't do fashion. I am fashion."*

ON SUCCESS & BUSINESS

- *"Don't spend time beating on a wall, hoping to transform it into a door."*
- *"Success is often achieved by those who don't know that failure is inevitable."*
- *"In order to be irreplaceable, one must always be different."*
- *"There are people who have money and people who are rich."*
- *"My life didn't please me, so I created my life."*

www.ingramcontent.com/pod-product-compliance
Lightning Source LLC
LaVergne TN
LVHW020433080526
838202LV00055B/5167